Snow w...

Snow White's Coffin

Kate Camp

Victoria University Press

VICTORIA UNIVERSITY PRESS
Victoria University of Wellington
PO Box 600 Wellington
vup.victoria.ac.nz

Copyright © Kate Camp 2013
First published 2013

This book is copyright. Apart from
any fair dealing for the purpose of private study,
research, criticism or review, as permitted under the
Copyright Act, no part may be reproduced by any
process without the permission of
the publishers.

National Library of New Zealand Cataloguing-in-Publication Data

Camp, Kate.
Snow White's coffin / Kate Camp.
ISBN 978-0-86473-888-2
I. Title.
NZ821.2—dc 23

Printed by PrintStop, Wellington

For Paul, with love

And for Karla Reimert, with memories
of our Wunderkammer evenings

Contents

. . . how is it possible to live when after all the elements of this life are utterly incomprehensible to us? If we are continually inadequate in love, uncertain in decision, and impotent in the face of death, how is it possible to exist?

Rainer Maria Rilke, letter to Lisa Heise, 8 November 1915

The loneliest ol' song in the world

i

If this song ever saw the light of day it would fade real quick.

This is the song of axes falling.
And I say this is the song of axes falling
axes falling across a river.

This is the song of an eyelid
of an eyelid and of lemonade
and oh my love, how I fell into that lemonade.

The song inside a snowglobe thinks
but it don't snow in Hawai'i
and then it starts and turns the surfboards all to cake.

ii

One night, broke in Nashville, Willie Nelson was scratching around his guitar looking to make the rent. Outside the window, lights were red, green and red again. And green. And he was thinking about his sister, his dead mom and dad and his grandparents' screen porch door, its segmented negative Milky Way studded with flattened insects. He was thinking about the future, how it would be different, would smell of different sauces, *so many freaking sauces*, he was thinking. And it was then that he stumbled upon this song, the loneliest ol' song in the world. And I'd like to sing that to you now.

iii

Sweetheart when the axe is falling on that river
I am the sound that travels slow across the water
I am the runaway hiding in the forest
The petite forest called your hair and heart.

Sweetheart when time is falling in your eyes
That broken limb of time and tired bear
I am the one that wanders in the forest
And finds you in that forest, in the haunted forest of your hair.

Sweetheart when the snow is falling in your hand
I am the quiet bits of air it's falling through
And I am the quiet ground it's falling to
And I am the falling one and you are falling too.

On reading Gray's *Elegy Written in a Country Churchyard*

The morning air smells of leaves.
I see the paper in its plastic bag
the path overlaid with fine green moss
houses' windows white with curtains.

Beyond the neighbours' yard the hills
the white sphere of the spy station
and above, the white circle of the moon
about the same size.

★

I saw my father on film the other day.
He was whatever age I am now.
He raised his eyebrows, clasped his hands
behind his back. He bent his body from the waist

as a crane might, or one of those novelty birds
that sips like a metronome from the side of a glass.
He smiled and moved his eyes around,
showing this side of the whites, and the other side.

★

In the morning, on lovely mornings
when I step into that air
I expect to see a corpse
to be the one who discovers the body.

I can see it, face down on the neighbours' lawn
one arm above its head
its knee bent
as if climbing a wall of grass.

I look up to the hills
over where the dead body is not
to the spy base, the spider's egg
with the moon above it.

I don't want to leave this world.

This is the well

Animals made of animal skin, made of lamps
Golden rams, milk-rabbits and horses of earthenware
Horses of bronze. What is that sky, eating up its birds?
What is that language, tasting the poison of its letters?
This is the well in which the water was drowned in buckets
The rope, the screeching handle, the grey mouth of sky.
This is the stable where the fire was housed, the fury
In its manger, its nest of straw-gold hair.

Oh my dear, the world would eat up its favourites.
Unconfined, bees flew their painful honey home
Spiders known only by their jewelly webs.
There were animals inside animals, and upon them
And most astute of all, the pig, saw the world
In the quick mirror of a knife.

Eye that is swallowed

Open this side of flesh – let's say of Christ –
Like a purse pack of tissues, layers of body
Of *person* in a limited palette of page, binding,
night accident, golden writing.
Beyond doubt, you become the eye that is swallowed
That you might travel punctual locations
Of anatomy, of the nineteenth century,
The pearl grey dawns of that found-out mystery.

Sweetheart, come into my body, said the dark
A voice within the orange grove
Within the ancient walls, protected by UNESCO.
Inside unmissable monuments of Europe
Inside the peopled church, the ordinary folks
Look up all at once, baring their throats.

The sea is dark and we are told it's deep

Inside these caverns dark and bloody only one man goes
with pickaxe and leather kit he tunnels
to produce the loudest man-made sound on the planet.
Earth flies like terrified geese
drummers burst drums, simple folks
hold their faces in astonishment.

These are the things we were not supposed to know:
that instants would expand to take up whole rooms,
and buildings, prison buildings, occupy our bodies.
The sliding and clanging of doors yes the sounds of captivity
just as they are in the movies, and we are looking back
over our heartbroken shoulders, me with my cut-up clothes
you with that scab on your lip, black and oval as a cockroach.

I sleep in your arms, as a half-built office tower
rests in the reach of a locked-up crane.

There is no easy way

This is the way you will travel through the world
on feet, on arrangements of bones and body parts.

You will be standing on top of your shoes.
You will be walking inside the lining of your coat
and your fingers will poke through the frayed pocket lining.

Around the islands of your back teeth, rich with metals,
will be the liquids that you drink, disappearing down your throat.

There will be air inside you, an egg of it
inside your mouth, and a clam of it.

When you lie in the dark you will be nothing but a clock
spending your limited supply of minutes on minutes.
You will always be inside things, be they rooms, buildings,
or atmospheres, because there is no *outside*.

And I will tell you something, you will have animals inside you.
Two dark, dark bears, sleeping in a reek of their own urine.
Swans caught with their wings open like fountains.
And there will be raccoons, black eyes full of night time.
They feed on rubbish when they can't find a home in the woods.

Everything is a clock

Across the floor she went
it was made of sawed-up trees
and patterned with the places branches grew.

All around, light was travelling at the speed of light
back and forth, and in the machine of the eye
was processed into a living knowledge

that was how movement occurred
bones and solid limbs carried through space
as a great crane outside the window

slowly swung a can of wet cement.
She travelled downwards in measured amounts
one head lower, one head lower

time as lived by a clock, as raison d'être.
Up she went, one head higher at a time
until born onto the street, not sure

if on the ground was leaves
or dappled chewing gum
or something altogether new

the animal markings of the earth
as it showed its coat
to the sky.

To myself

Precisely in the manner of Marcus Aurelius
I remain below the covers. You don't know this
how they smell of washing liquid

hold warmth in themselves as a body
that when I return from the kitchen
I open them as a body

they are not eating me they are not having sex
with me they are not giving birth to me
but they are a body for me and I for them

an item from that body
perhaps a thumb held within its hand
or two feet that keep each other company in the night.

Here within our clothes within our bedclothes
in our eyes our hairs and skins within this air
this particular envelope of air which might be made of space

except that it is made of time.
There are cooler patches of sheet to which I can apply
the inside of my knee.

I will put my hand beneath my ear
my eye will adhere to that place on the eyelid
that ancient injury, that when I wake

the fear of pain will make me hold the eyeball still
and not pursue a thought, a leaping deer.
The body is a coward, that is its job

to suck from the world its sugars
crawl into the slain bodies of monsters,
if necessary, to find a place to sleep.

A living example

for Stefanie Lash

She is a girl with a beautiful shoulder
that much I can tell you
and an arm, as the arm in a statue
takes up space in its whiteness
that is the space her arm and shoulder occupy
her red lips, the lips of a spy
that is how mysterious she's become
as she takes down the secret messages of despair.

If you want to be a player in space
you have to overcome the rendezvous problem
how, with nothing to push up against,
one must bring the great, heavy ship to port.

That is what she must conquer now.

★

Gold, inalterable metal, thus eternal,
is the matter that composes the flesh of the gods.

Their innards work as jewellery
precious stones and the machine that shows
within the egg made of cherries a single cherry
and within the cherry a pit made of gold.

None of that will help her now, ladies and gentlemen,
as she treads the carbon of the present.
You can't fault the planet for consistency
the way it can turn each night into a day
break each day down
into its composite hours.

These are the mechanisms she must work with now
must work within, must smash against her dumb face
as if handless, as if all fingers and thumbs given up
she wielded only clubby stumps in their stead.

★

She holds the warm black banister of an escalator,
one moving a little faster than the other
so that when she finds the top she might be
pulled open at the chest into a pose of great relief
or ripped, imperceptibly, in two.

Neither of these occurs. But she does reach Weyden's annunciation
in which Mary waves away the angel
with the gesture of one refusing flyers in the street.

One hundred and fifty-one thousand bridges

It seems unlikely that, in its progress past the yet unbuilt floor
of an apartment building, a bucket containing a broom and a spade
can block out the sun. I am always surprised

to see leaves fall from the sky, mistake them for birds,
or plastic bags. Do you sometimes feel you might be painted
onto the world, find yourself standing

like an angel in a Dutch interior, with nothing to do?
You hold your hands in poses
as if playing invisible instruments

can't help but see the sleeping signs
of still life: a pomegranate lying on its side
a knife, a board, a loaf of bread. Do you see the world

there, its green hills and brown villages hanging on the wall?
Who knows what is really inside what, the room a doll's house
or the world a box, open up the cardboard doors

at last the day has come to see into the tiny countryside!
Watch me move across this chessboard with my angel feet
from behind you see the soles

turned backward like two lumbering beasts
far across a prairie.
History is taking place inside me, all its waste

young men exploding into trees
mining for silver and building bridges,
one hundred and fifty-one thousand bridges

Kutno

You can never describe
what you see from the windows of trains.

The red, circular sun, as if this greying evening
were the tropics.

Restless birds
circling and washing overhead

scattering and gathering themselves
in silhouette.

Stopped at Kutno. Our very stillness
makes us seem to slide quietly backwards.

Perhaps we are that ceaseless boat
and these black birds the current

but look, they are stopping now
their heavy shapes inhabit the leafless trees

as in a picture. This is a diagram of the world,
this world.

Letter to a friend

The milk has frozen solid
its carton swelled like a pillow
and what you can pour from it, as it melts
is a thin white water.

I thought about you yesterday.
The park was full of children
barely visible in the dark
on thin poles they carried their lanterns
each with no flame inside
but small torches
bought by their parents for the purpose
or lightsticks, like pencils of colour.

One girl had lost her mother,
I left her by the tree she said,
as we looked into the invisible park
the greatest in this side of the city
built over a mountain of bunkers
that were smashed and filled with rubble
once the war was over.

We stood stamping while policemen stopped the traffic.
The carol-singing never started
but we walked back through the park
just the three of us
and Karla and Magdelena sang
and fully-clothed joggers
loomed out of, and back into, the mist.

After pizza we had bubble tea
the bubbles come up thick straws
like roe, you pop the sweet strawberry caviar
between your tongue and the roof of your mouth
the roof, as if the body were a building.
We all had the same feeling,
as if we were drinking the future.

It wasn't the future of course. It was the past. This is all the past.
That is why I can tell you about it:
because I crushed it in my mouth and destroyed it.

And thus concludes my letter. May I only add
that at the time I thought of you
the ground was thick with leaves
not yellow ones anymore, just soft and brown
like the patchy coat of an animal.

Everybody has to be somewhere

i

Not so much a wind blowing
as a large and steady quantity of space
arriving and arriving
from a much colder location.

I see the moon sometimes from this bus route
appearing between houses
for five or ten seconds at a time.

I know the road so well but I only ever walked along it once,
I was going to meet my mother, that mythical creature,
and I walked in my dark green imagination
and breathed air and listened to a conversation
actually took my headphones out just to listen.

Of course I can't remember what they were saying now
or who they were, or who I was. I was a little bit a child,
because as a child I walked past many white
suburban railings, and I was a little bit a young woman
because I felt something of a fool.
Mainly, though, I was an adult woman
who will notice the smell of leaves, if it's on offer.

ii

There is so much I will never be,
I knew as I walked between those walls of stone.
And I can never go back, am ripped from the past
as unkindly as the scabs were ripped
from the soft side of a Brontë sister in the story
of their lives, the way Mum told it anyway.

Of everything that is, at any time, there is so much that isn't.
The world is said to be overcrowded
but when I fly I seem to fly over so much wilderness.

The film might have been the new Mike Leigh
or about the persecution of French Jews.
My mother might have been wearing
a dark green – but she never wears dark green – a dark green
          cardigan.
I don't know. I know I walked there
through a day, through the stony passageway.
And when I got there my mother was still alive.
And I was still alive.

iii

Across the road, they are building an apartment block.
Every day you see them in there, behind a green tree
and then through a yellow one. I saw one of them hold
a sheet of plywood, the size of a door, as if ballroom dancing.

To think that all this world has been made by hand.
A man's eye has looked not only onto walls
but into them, and each of those rusted sheets of metal squares
that lie inside poured concrete, those bones have been seen
and settled down into the grey.
And that, across this city, this *continent.*
There is so much of everything.

Snow White's Coffin

Tom Waits records the sound of frying chicken
that's how he achieves his pops and crackles.
Our old unit had a hooked grey arm,
it was a trunk of wood with woven speakers.

As a child I worried about forgetting:
the hexagonal handle, a creamy honey cell,
that flaw in the lino resembling Donald Duck
while the others of its kind looked like grey bells.

Sometimes life would seem too big, even then
an empty Sunday where you drifted as a ghost.
I saw *Bonnie and Clyde* on such a day,
as I recall, in black and white

when the bullets came
they died like oceans
full of slow turbulence
as if brought by death to life.

Why preserve one's childhood memories?
So, like Egyptians, they might be packed into the grave?
That I would sit up nights, eating from the Haworth mug
spoonfuls of plain sugar mixed with cinnamon.

Is there room in the sarcophagus for that,
for the feeling of the covers of paperbacks,
in which girls survive, among great trees,
girls who make mistakes in forests.

One thing I loved was to pick the scabs on my knees
while sitting on the toilet.
Do I need to say, I ate them?
Who is taking this down?

★

The Dutch I believe, have built a car one molecule long.
I've seen its silly form, its atom wheels.
It looks nothing like a car, it looks to be a pupa
some kind of baby bee surprised by disaster in its cell.

The problems of this world will not be solved by tiny cars.
Everything is small enough already
and there is too much, too much of everyone.
To understand your life you need another whole life.

I think we are sitting here on the axis my friend
that is why we feel a bit unwell.
Buried in us are minutes, days, mornings slept late
nights of no rest, turning to one side

turning again like a tide
sweating into the bodies of hot beds
those bucketfuls of moisture.
I think that futures might be in us too

driving in tiny cars, they are opening their minute glove
boxes and with infinitesimal hands
draw out maps too small to imagine
but they imagine them, they look at the lists of streets

all arranged according to the alphabet.
And then I think they throw the book away.
And they get out from the car
and they throw the keys into the ocean

howling. They do not want to go to places in books.
They will not drive
in their molecule cars
those ridiculous cartoons.

★

Snow White's Coffin
is an integrated radio and record player
that introduced Plexiglas to the domestic interior.
Relieve yourself of the excruciating clutter of the world

is what it says to you
everything you thought was *being alive*
is revealed as a problem
which can be solved by good design.

Self-adhesive horror stickers

Grey sickles, speckled with blood
for your convenience. Some eggs will be patterned
this way, the eggs of Middle European songbirds.

Day appears upon its stage
a Bakelite green gently usurping the dark.

To wake in a landscape made of people
appearing from the earth as bulbs
as signposts will, pointing their fingers at crossroads.

The body made in particular order
may be unmade in a treasury of ways
as when you sweep into your paw
the grey nubby hands of a jigsaw.

You can buy a three-dimensional wound
to stick on your arm like a little bloody cunt

though the one boy I know
went to Halloween as a doctor
with a heart inside a jar.

Galileo's law of falling bodies

A grey world looms behind as backdrop.
That is what it is to belong to a place,
to be built of its material, never able to rip away a foot
a hand, and walk off with your bloody hams showing.

I dream sometimes of hornets, I know a way to kill them
but the poison won't spray properly
runs warmly down my wrist and arm,
between my fingers.

We stop in amazement in front of things
a woman with a castle on her head
but it is us who are amazing
with our planet made of pronouns.

I leave you now, rise up from the marble bathroom
and when I step outside that's not enough
and so I leave the city, and I go where fields of metal poles
are ranged in a musical matrix

that's not enough, shut down my eyes
I see the red and then the navy blue of blackness
I step into that cup, that cut
you know what's coming next.

When I gaze on the celestial globe
I see stars marked as bullet holes
I see the centaur
an entry wound on his muscled throat.

Double glazing

Once it is dark, there is no exterior.
Night becomes a means of reflection
you see room upon golden room
all in slightly wrong formation.

Something about light, about its properties
and the eye, which almost knows this, almost can
discern how this wall could be behind itself
a shadow and companion, that doors

which once by day appeared to open outward
start to open inward and within themselves
within again. You have seen a flower bloom in time lapse:
that is how doors are behaving in the window.

If people are to enter such a room, actual people,
they of course become their second selves. They loom
not out of darkness, but from a light so come-from-nowhere
it appears to be a darkness.

As they approach from the right they are seen from the left
and from the left the right, the *right*
as if one direction would always be
the home of knowledge.

When you maintain your watch
through night's medium
sized hours, blue morning comes.
This is what light will do:

Slowly take away the room
destroy its layers, its unexpected angles
its demonstrations of the laws of light and how light falls
and how the eye performs its tasks of understanding.

And so, when day is fully here, the window will be empty
that dolls' house theatre, that gold confusion
gone. There will only be the so-called outside world
going about its business made of sound.

History as seen through the eyes of babies

The dataset of the future:
What babies saw, in their orbits.

How their thoughts were outside windows
their thoughts were clouds passing by windows.

Their literature, barking of dogs in courtyards
faint songs transmitted through floorboards.

The history of babies is the history of people, rising and circling
as planets do.

As with the history of grown men
this history, history

as seen through the eyes of babies
is not without its grand conundrums

why death arrived too late
so long after everyone was born

and why the oceans, soft and woollen,
had never been harvested for their fur.

Memory of the future

night time

I sit on the octagonal table
as on a grey honey cell

huge black trees   with wings
as black as   black birds' wings

are not there

dunes are small hills   made of sand
sand that by night   appears grey

while by daylight   it is grey

you don't know how cool it can be
how hot

in the future, everyone has died

the present tense
is all that remains

behind me   where I am not

an iron fence   curved   like a wave of sound

a scarecrow
a dog, lunging on its chain

I look up   let the old, tired light
settle on my face   like a sheet

Rendering synthetic objects into legacy photographs

First, understand light's direction
does it enter the room from a window
arrowing down from the ancient past?
Understand what light will do

what it knows
about you, about the table
and the picture of Hokusai's great wave
what it knows about colour

how colour will reflect
from this suddenly inserted Chinese dragon
to make the ceiling slightly rosy.
Measure the depth of everything

estimate the light, and the albedo light
that's the light that no one understands, the light
that makes you look like a person
not like a mannequin, falling, falling.

Here a glowing sphere illuminates the room
reflecting in mirrors and casting shadows.
Don't you wish you had lived long enough to see this,
this golden ball appear in the motel bedroom

its mini sun passing the made-up bed
transiting the folds of the curtain
the small white fridge, the motel pen
and pad with only seven pages.

You might have rested your dark head
on that pillow while, above,
the sphere hovered
like a curious bee.

The award-winning map

Only a human man would know
to shade the boundaries

with a soft green lip
and show the airport

its name curved as a rainbow
while ignoring several nearby towns.

Not a body organ, as you first suspect
but a lake.

He has marked in dotted lines
the paths of ferry crossings.

He has shaded in the mountains
that you might look across a nation

and understand
as you would the shape, beneath the bedclothes,

of an ailing relative;
not perfectly

but enough to know
this is where the foot rises

here the noble peak
of its sideways leaning toes

here the leg
the Black Hills

their pines pointing always upwards
as on prison garb.

Lupa

On a morning you may find yourself
head as level as a glass of water
an abundance of air everywhere it should be:
circulating behind your eyes, filling your body
as the curved breasts of a sail.

You carry your coat, it is true,
but not as a burden, as an elegant aside
it falls from your hand with folds
of light and dark. You move through the world
as one whose three dimensions mark
the very hour in which realism reached its peak.

I run my hands over the grubby plaster model
of Botticelli's Venus installed for the enjoyment of the blind.
Followed by students in blue uniform I pass by many works
in which the heads of saints lie on golden records.

The outside world is shown in a passageway of windows:
trees the shape of bay leaves
the slow dirty river shining upwards.

So often you see a statue
the label says it held a snake
or shows in dotted lines the body reach its hand
towards a now long-shattered piece of fruit.
I recall one crouching woman
her back bore just an infant hand,
an exquisitely rendered scab.

One hears in wartime how the body will be rendered into pieces
with no shape, pieces of body that have only weight.
Here is one, red marble, the size of the largest suitcase
you may take onto a plane
muscle rolling in its landscape
full of power but unable to be understood.

Who would know this from a rock?
Could even the best trained animal
foraging the ruins of a city
find this as a living form?
I want to touch it, but the guard woman is watching on.

Down the hallway a special light is shining
it's the light that comes in windows
when a woman turns her head
as a radar dish turns in its white egg cover.

Every piece of art I see from now
will just destroy a piece of art I've seen before
so instead I eat a sandwich, the kind of sandwich
I would never eat at home: just meat, thin meat,
it has a familiar tone, like the meat of someone you know.
I sit in the sun and eat while pigeons patrol the battlements.

Spreepark

for Gaby Lingke

We stood in a small field
among winter-dead yellow grass
the sun was shining on us from above
and we were casting no shadow
at least, the shadow we cast was beneath us
a pool, a root, a base, on which we were safe.

Taking up a lot of sky was the ferris wheel.
I didn't know then, but it would start to turn
in the wind, and make a sound
like the distant call from a muezzin.
As it turned through its circle
its red metal structures made a constant lesson
in geometry as the area of sky
within each shape gave itself over to the next.

A man walked his son towards the toilet
then stopped by the bushes
and pulled down the little boy's warm pants
so he could piss in the open air.
Later the same boy, with his small spade,
walked past staring up at me
he wondered why I stood, perhaps,
in the small grass field, looking at nothing,
what to him was nothing, the slow-moving wheel
and its companion, the chimney
creating and creating a roiling white cloud
like a time-lapse of the weather
a pure, mesmerised pollution
utterly at home in an empty blue sky.

All the broken-down rides, the Grand Canyon
boats filled with leaves, the fallen dinosaurs
cars with ears, and the mouth of a cat
into which the rollercoaster disappeared:
you know about those. What you don't know
is that, in the small field, there are hedges
only knee high, and beyond them, behind a fence
the white shape that appears to be a mammoth
a broken mammoth, or a work in progress.
Trees leaning up against the sky like twiggy brooms.

It is true, many disasters may befall the human eye.
How can it be that we must walk through a world
with this little gelid world to lead us?
I thought you brought a telescope today
but it's your great aunt's tripod, in its leather tube.
We are none of us sailors but I look to the horizon
above the kiosk and the heads of dog owners
waiting for the tour to begin, beyond the river
where the great chimney, alone,
is speaking its clouds into the sky.
We understand, you and I, that sunshine
is a form of time
and we stand in the small field
and watch it pass by.

The Sleeping Fury

i

The best statues are present on chill evenings
when, in the courtyard, a white camellia bows its flowers
and hides its botanical label in dark, shining leaves.

Statues holding their heads
in their arms, in helmets, like loaves of bread.
Statues that are copies of other statues
that aren't even real, statues that may be restored
according to contemporary ideals of beauty.

The best statues are being seen by the woman
whose hair is grey at the front but white at the back
the woman who must look in two mirrors
to really understand what is happening with her head.

At the top of a thin column appears the head of a boy
he looks to be school age but the head is smaller than life size
a foetus-sized head of a grown-up boy, a boy who says
I am four and ten quarters.

ii

I hear a lot about partial-birth abortion,
I don't know what it is. I listen to too much American
politics when I should be listening to classical music
I should be caring about classical music.

Head of a little boy, consecrated to Isis.
That's what the little boy head is called.

iii

I want to tell you about one more statue,
it lay on a plinth as you lie on a floor when,
driven by despair onto the ground, or simply tired out
you lay yourself onto a flat hard surface.
You don't find a pillow. You don't even rest upon your arm
on its cluster of muscles and mechanisms,
but lay your head flat down, as the face lies on a stamp.

This sculpture has been interpreted at various times
as a Sleeping Fury or a Medusa. When it was in the Cesi
Collection it was identified as a water nymph
and placed on a marble cushion.
When it entered the Ludovisi Collection
the left side of the face was cut horizontally
to improve the stability of the piece.
The head is now believed to be
a second-century Roman copy,
perhaps a wounded Amazon.

The world's most impractical machine

The world's most impractical machine
only functions on the incoming tide
brown foam, and posts, relics of a former fence:
these are what power the machine.

Its purpose, put simply, alleviation of pain
through creation of other, more succulent pain.
It records, in its chambers,
what you look upon at time of death

upon pebbles white, clouds on the move
upon ceilings' small and perfect craters
that inverse braille, walls where windows
hang like paintings, or curtains closed

on the theatre of the world. Of course, ninety-nine
per cent of records show the underside
of eyelids, that is, the constellations
orbiting the human eye.

The machine must be in constant motion
so is built upon a curving base
to trump the laws of physics
or demonstrate them, I suppose.

You have seen a time-lapse film of building
how the crane turns here and there
scaffolding fluttering up as all the while the sun
flops wildly from one side of the sky to the other:

such is the functioning of the world's most impractical machine,
what is slow, it does quickly, and in doing so makes the monumental
temporary. It's all about time, the machine, about how time,
like everything else, gets overtaken by time.

I don't know what happened to the posts.
Did the sand arrive to bury them layer by layer
or the ocean undermine the base of them
and draw them out, horizontal, on the tide?

A living body is never really calm

I searched and searched
for the freezing point of water
but was constantly directed
to the melting point.

That can happen, when you approach your life
from both ends, rushing to its centre
where your damaged eyes
settle on a shared location.

You put a lion in a cage, see the wings of a fly
in all their glory. You make contact with the ground
over and over, each time the same heels
strike the earth as hammers:

no wonder parts of you are numb, as if dying ahead of time,
no wonder parts of you must be removed
you are being mined, not for precious metals
but for failures.

At the museum of artificial limbs
the oh-so-articulate body. Every time you trip
you lift your knee. Not even a spaceship
can stop itself from falling the way you do.

The kids experiment with human fear,
it makes it hard to walk across the canyon
even when the canyon isn't there, even when it disappears
and turns into a waterfall.

Nuns

I think I see nuns in restaurants.
It's a recognised phenomenon
caused by the black-and-white staff
folding and flapping tablecloths.

When I actually do see nuns
whatever they are doing surprises me.
Oh look, a nun on a bicycle, I think.
Or, huh. A nun in an airport.

When you live in a cell
you might have a view of a tree
as Anne Frank did
or a view of the inner cloister.

You are not *of* the world
that's the theory.
But what preposition operates
between *you* and *world*?

Maybe you are *with* the world
you accompany it
as one might go with a friend
to a medical appointment.

In the monastery of San Marco
Jesus walked from his cave
carrying a pickaxe. Sometimes miracles
are achieved by hand.

Sometimes miracles are achieved
by the human body.
The white neck of the virgin
thick and muscular as a thigh.

The night sky on any day in history

I want you to look into an oncoming night.
Is it a little green? Does it have the cool orange
beginnings of streetlights? Tip your head back
as someone with a nosebleed might.
Survey the lower sky. Are there chimneys
making mini city silhouettes? Satellite dishes,
their smooth, grey craters turned in one direction?

You might insist you hear a nightingale.
Might see, at a distance, the huge screen
advertising an upcoming concert by the Beach Boys.
You could spend your time watching trains pull
their strings of yellow windows along in lines.

Or you might come here, where I am
where I stand upon the rarely silent floor
looking up at the rectangle moon
of our neighbour's window.

Interrupted world

You, neighbour,
waving your yellow towel

turning it into a yellow shirt
that you dress yourself in.

You fold your arms
or swing them like a signalman.

Can you imagine how your face might feel
to the air? How the hot summer wind

might shape itself around your blue-bruised calf
or the violet landscape of your hand veins?

The trees are giving off asterisks
pollinating you by accident.

And when the black military vehicle of a beetle
finds its way onto your skirt.

And when boats, travelling under bridges
are pushing heavy, empty barges.

And when dogs tremble
as they hover over their business in parks.

Death of a princess

You see Princess Diana
pass through that grey revolving door
over and over.

On the corner here, you can buy a coffin.
You can buy a polystyrene urn, with a silver anchor,
avail yourself of an airplane, find

contentment between earth and sky.
There were lampposts here, in the wintertime
as huge as pictures of lamps. Now there are trees, impenetrable

trees and the stone of the building, falling away
but it's not stone, I know, it's plaster
plaster over brick. Somehow more astonishing to think

that such a world may be made of little loaves.
You look up, a woman at a window.
White curtain, its leisurely surrender.

The fall of 1981

The fall of 1981
as if a year may be an empire.

It is not true to say that every year is a life
born in spring, born in winter

in a summer morning where a chrome container
sits on the windowsill full of ashes.

And every day is not a lifetime
where you travel smooth into death

listening to accounts of the brain
which is always to blame

and the corn that covers America
in a yellow armour.

Your body is not a planet
not a galaxy peppered with old

mistakes you can't even remember the names of.
Whole dimensions go AWOL

though you recall
this bad moustache, and the laugh under it

as Buster drank beer from the carpet
or such and such a smashed side mirror, and a plum

and the recurring smell of shoes
pulled white with mildew from a wardrobe.

Birds don't have a song, they make a sound
you might as well say

the song of breaking glass
the song of doors.

One by one I am eating up the seasons.
I mean, one by one the seasons are eating me up.

It would be easy to say that I go where ventriloquists'
dummies go when ventriloquists die.

But oh! There you are at your window again
you pull back your white curtain

and say |yeah|
to someone I don't know about.

The great [or perhaps vast] night

When the aliens came
they unfolded themselves
in the way we knew they would
with a threatening economy of movement
as everything they needed to destroy us was contained
within everything they needed to find us, to travel to us.

Notices were issued in the native language
about supplies of food that would need to be accumulated.

In cafés, cafeterias in fact, we smoked and ate pistachios
letting the shells fall clacking onto tables like fingernails.
And our cigarettes, which we had long before abandoned,
their orange brown butts lay everywhere
like the crushed funnels of ships.

As I walked with you through the abandoned factory
along its open galleried walkways
and above and below its concrete levels
there was the ever-present fear of the great machines
but also, a ridiculous sense of optimism
as we surveyed the containers of food
knowing in our hearts that they would rot and spoil
and be useless and yet and yet . . .
they stood upon each other in towers.

And we had put so much stock in such a small number of stories
that when it came to it,
we could only invoke the same old characters.

In a quiet yellow-lit underground carpark
we sat reading from the old books.

The books that had never imagined this
had imagined us, they knew us
as we rode in our emeralds over vast estates.
The god of the north wind with snakes for feet.
Noah whose name meant comfort and whose name meant rest.

And this one here, this woman inside a carriage
this woman in her carpet-walled anteroom
in the staircase of the backstage of the ballet and here
I found her again in this story
she turns up her ear to the light of the star.

That is what she was reading when the end came.
When the aliens unfolded their machines
or you could say unfolded themselves, for the final time.

The call of death

I call you with my hand.
I only have one hand.
I only am one hand.

In the palm is where I do my thinking.

As they say a sailor plays out a rope '
I play you in.

The Dalai Lama when a boy
was kept secret as an owl.

I will be that room
with no exits and entrances
with no windows
with no walls no roof and no floor.

Death is recognised as a friend

I knew you as the one who had placed birds
in places where birds might not be –
in the cool lightwell of the hotel
among the laundry; or on the sky
as a kind of momentary lettering.

Your authorship was everywhere:
in the close but never to be touching hands
of figures in ancient paintings
and in the smell of burning
that came up from the subway
and the grooved black-and-silver stairs of the escalator
vanishing neatly into their combs.

Woman confiding in death

Sometimes I feel my body expand
I am heavy in every direction.
I dream that I am drunk
too drunk to walk or speak
and I crawl along the dream earth.

Is it possible to be a great, unwieldy vessel
made of dense material, hollow,
and somehow still be rising
as if drawn into an empty sky by gravity?

I could have been a scientist
the kind who gives names
to the members of a group of wolves.
I could have been a ship, making my effortful sounds
underwater.

Soul

A singer, moving
in the best traditions of soul

as if under the affliction of some comical
tragical disease. Outside the window

three women in headscarves pass
like three wise men in caravan.

There might be a day when all this is no more.
That day is today. That day is tomorrow.

Once your eyes adjust to the dark
you realise you are surrounded by dancers

you are surrounded by singers
you are standing under the sign of the fleeing man

making his way from the green world
through the green door into the green outside.

Caspar, Melchior and Balthazar.
I just wanted to say that.

Untitled poem about my neighbours

My neighbours,
dear neighbours
your *interiors*
hung on the dark like paintings

each window a crucifix
here with a candle burning, here
the solitary lightning
of the television.

I don't want to know you but I want to know you
are there, trying on your red top
before the mirror.

And I want to hear you make mistakes
when you gather your friends round the piano.

I came up in a cage lift once, not here,
somewhere less efficient,
and I waited dumbstruck on the landing
by piano music from above
while in my hand the cold
carton of milk wept real tears.

I admit I watch you naked
your pale breasts
evoking all the *Playboy*s of my youth.

I never saw *Inception*
but I saw the city – it was Paris – turn in upon itself.
We've done that too

and though it took me years to see it
there's a kind of Sphinx
at the foot of the stairs
a dark green woman
with wings and claws

and there's the smell of the cellar
that basement smell
we are living on earth, then, after all.

Berlin

Echoes, sounds of keys, you collect your mail
in the courtyard like a call to prayer.

In peripheral vision the chamber of the lift comes down
these glass towers are added on to all the buildings.

I know things about doors and windows.
About the neck, what it can endure

on the rollercoasters of historic Europe.
And I know about streets, their dangers

and the synagogues they hold, gold above the traffic.
I am putting on my wooden heart.

I am donning the jewellery of forgiveness.
I make sounds with the bones of my body

like some private machine.
You can sit for hours here over empty plates

a privileged cave man
by the picked over remnants of a bone.

And when you finish your drink,
you just stand the bottle up on the street.

There's broken glass everywhere.

Notes

The epigraph is from *Letters of Rainer Maria Rilke – Volume II: 1910–1926*, translated by Jane Bannard Greene and M.D. Herter Norton (W.W. Norton, 1945).

'The sea is dark and we are told it's deep' is a line from John Berryman's 1938 poem 'Conversation'.

'This is the well' and 'Eye that is swallowed' are from a series of sonnets written in response to the work of other poets; these two are in response to Paul Celan and Miroslav Holub, respectively.

'To myself' is the title Marcus Aurelius gave to the writings that later became known as his Meditations.

'Everybody has to be somewhere' is the punch line of a Henny Youngman joke, as told in Paul Auster's novel *Leviathan* (Viking, 1992): a man finds a man is hiding in his closet; he asks what he's doing there and the man in the closet replies, 'Everybody has to be somewhere.'

The title and final stanza of 'The Sleeping Fury' are taken verbatim from the English label in the museum of the Ludovisi Collection in Rome.

'The great [or perhaps vast] night' is a line from one of William Gass's translations of Rilke's Duino Elegies, in *Reading Rilke: Reflections on the Problems of Translation*, William H. Gass (Knopf, 1999).

'The call of death', 'Death is recognised as a friend', and 'Woman confiding in death' are titles of works by Käthe Kollwitz.

Acknowledgements

I am very grateful to Creative New Zealand for awarding me the Berlin Writer's Residency, which enabled me to write this book.

Thanks to the Goethe-Institut Wellington, for generously providing private German lessons before I took up the residency, and to my teacher Emma Thoenißen.

I had great support from the New Zealand Embassy in Berlin, which helped me make valuable contacts in the city.

Thanks to Erica Duthie and Struan Ashby, with whom I co-created a project at the 2012 Frankfurt Book Fair, and to the team involved in New Zealand's guest of honour programme at the Fair.

My writing group workshopped these poems with their usual insight and kindness, and our weekly online meetings across the time zones were a real treat. Thanks Hinemoana Baker, Stefanie Lash, Maria McMillan and Marty Smith.

I learned so much and took so much inspiration from Karla Reimert's German translation of my previous book, *The Mirror of Simple Annihilated Souls*. Working together on that poet-to-poet translation was an exhilarating experience. Thank you Karla.

Most of all, thank you to my friends in Berlin for helping me feel at home in the city, and find my way in the German language: Lisa Futschek, Alva Gehrmann, Damien Harrison, Birgit Hunkenschroer, Friederike Kämper, Gaby Lingke, Karla Reimert, Mattias Seidenstücker and Tania Wehrs.